Where Do I Go Now, God?

RESTLESS HEARTS

Studies for Young Adults

Where Do I Go Now, God?

study & reflection guide

Alex Joyner

ABINGDON PRESS / Nashville

RESTLESS HEARTS
WHERE DO I GO NOW, GOD?
Study & Reflection Guide

ISBN 978-0-687-33546-6

07 08 09 10 11 12 13 14 15 16—10 9 8 7 6 5 4 3 2 1
MANUFACTURED IN THE UNITED STATES OF AMERICA

CONTENTS

INTRODUCTION

RESTLESS HEARTS
WHERE DO I GO NOW, GOD?

Welcome to Restless Hearts, a small group study for young adults that will help you reflect upon who you are, upon what you want to do with your life, and upon God's presence and care for you in the midst of your vocational journey. As you participate in this vocational reflection study, you will:

- gain a sense of God's care for you
- understand more about your own personality, identity, and gifts
- discover that a relationship with God is the primary vocation of all people
- view your life work and education or training necessary for that work in light of God's purposes

- develop spiritual disciplines of prayer, Bible study, and personal reflection
- discover the value of and insights gained by participating with others in a small-group setting
- experience the freedom to explore some of your deepest questions and concerns regarding vocation and faith during this particular stage of your life
- discover ways to help others as you search for purpose and meaning in your life.

Core Values

The small group study is grounded in the following values, which you will review in each of the six sessions:

- We are created to be related to God and others.
- Our vocation is more than our job.
- Baptism is the continuing reminder of who we are.
- Our careers should work in concert with our vocation, not against it.
- The key career question is not, "What do I want to do for the rest of my life?" but, "Who am I, and what am I going to do next?"
- We discern our path by paying attention to the world around us and to what is happening within us.
- Spiritual disciplines help us discern God's calling.

"Our Heart Is Restless"

"For you have made us for yourself, and our heart is restless until it rests in you."[1] The name of this study was prompted by these words of Augustine of Hippo (354–430), a North African bishop in the early church who found his vocation and sense of self through an examination of his life. Augustine's emphasis on self-reflection is most evident in his autobiographical work, *The Confessions of Saint Augustine*. Here he begins with the affirmation that is central to the Restless Hearts approach to vocational reflection. God has created us in such a way that we cannot fully understand ourselves apart from God. Since we often live our lives with an incomplete awareness of how we are related to God, we are discontented. Augustine encourages us to pay attention to the inner tuggings that pull us toward God, a condition he describes as having a restless heart.

At the same time that Augustine recognized how central his relationship to God was for him, he also knew that other relationships were important as well. In his *Confessions,* he walks back through his life retelling it in such a way that he sees the contributions his mother, his teachers, and even children playing in a neighboring garden made to his vocational understanding. All of the parts of his life, even the parts he was not very proud of, were moments he could reclaim as times when God was present in the midst of relationships drawing him toward a new vision of who he was.

One of Augustine's lasting legacies is his emphasis on self-reflection as a means to understanding God. The journey toward God is one that passes through the interior life of each person. This study follows the example of St. Augustine in looking at vocation through our identities as children of God through Jesus Christ. It is a Christian study that assumes that God is present in and calls all persons through their explorations of vocation. Who are we? Who did God create us to be? How does God want us to live? What are we to do with our lives? All the sessions invite you to consider these questions and others.

Session One, "Inside Out: Expectations," will help you identify the tensions that exist between your inner sense of values and calling and the expectations that others have for you. You will explore the benefits of listening for God both inside and outside of yourself as a part of the lifelong process of vocational discernment.

Session Two, "Passion and Vocation," will help you recognize that the passions that drive us are often unacknowledged and sometimes unappreciated. Uncovering your passion, that is, what your heart truly desires, is one way to listen for God and to explore vocation. The session invites you to listen to your passion as a way of listening to God.

Session Three, "Trusting the Gifts," will help you move to a deeper level of trust that there is a purpose moving through your gifts. It encourages you to claim your gifts and abilities as you identify your vocation.

Session Four, "Listening in the Shadows," will help you recognize that a vocational journey oriented toward God may lead you to despise or suppress those parts of yourself you feel are unworthy or unnecessary. However, there are treasures to be found when you search among your needs, anxieties, and places of brokenness for God's healing presence. You will be encouraged to explore the role that our "shadow side" plays in helping us listen for God.

Session Five, "Somebody's Calling Your Name," will help you discover that you can also claim your vocation as you meet God in the needs of the world. It encourages you to identify needs in the world around you that are crying out for response and to develop a pattern of engaging in acts of service and justice.

Session Six, "Taking Risks," will help you discover that risk is an invaluable tool for moving from who you have been to who you are going to be. By consciously choosing to stretch yourself into areas where you know you will be required to change, you can experience greater trust in God and greater awareness of God's call. This final session provides the tools for identifying an action plan for your next steps in the vocational journey.

Format for the Sessions

Each session includes the following sequence of activities:

Opening Worship: Each week when the group gathers, you will begin with a worship experience. Restless Hearts *Where Do I Go Now, God?* uses stones and water to remind you of baptism as a symbol of your identity as a beloved member of God's family.

The Questions: This section offers stories and illustrations in the workbook and 8–10-minute video segments that will invite you to engage the focus for each week's study through personal reflection and small group discussion.

The Scriptures: Each session will explore specific biblical texts related to the session focus. The workbook contains a box entitled "Your Reflections on the Scriptures." You will respond to the questions in this box each week as an important part of your personal reflection.

Your Life: You will reflect upon your life and the Core Values that ground the study in a variety of activities included in this segment. The workbook contains a box entitled "Core Values and Your Life." You will respond to the questions in this box each week as another important part of your personal reflection.

Looking Ahead: This part of the session includes reading and journaling in the workbook. These activities will prepare you for the next session.

Closing Worship: Every session concludes with a worship experience related to the focus for the session.

Your Workbook

Your workbook contains stories, narratives, information, and questions that invite reflection and response. You will use it during the sessions and for your personal reflection between the sessions. You will also find space for writing in between sessions. You will notice boxes entitled "Your Reflections on the Scriptures" and "Core Values and Your Life." Each week you are invited respond to the questions in these boxes. In addition, the section entitled "Looking Ahead" suggests an activity for your personal reflection that will prepare you for the next session. The study invites you to adopt the discipline of journaling through the course of these sessions; however, responses in the workbook may take many forms, such as writing, drawing, use of symbols, or use of timelines. You may even treat the workbook as a kind of scrapbook to collect pictures or items that are meaningful to you as you respond to the exercises. What is most important is that you use the workbook to help you reflect on the session topics, the Scriptures, the Core Values of the study, and on your life.

Your Vocation

Let's return to the questions asked in the previous section entitled "Our Heart Is Restless," but this time we ask them in a slightly different way to make them more personal. Who am I? Who did God create me to be? How does God want me to live? What am I to do with my life? This study offers you a unique opportunity to explore your answers to these questions in the company of other young adults who are also asking these questions for themselves.

---

[1] *The Confessions of Saint Augustine,* translated by John K. Ryan (Doubleday, 1960); page 43.

1

Session One
Inside Out: Expectations

Opening Prayer

Bless to us, O God, this water—
from the waters of the womb
to journeys taken through stormy seas,
it is a reminder of your grace and promise.
Help us to walk with you.

Bless to us, O Christ, this group—
ready to explore and encounter
new callings and old.
Help us to walk with you.

Bless to us, Holy Spirit, this time—
ripe with potential
and full of your presence.
Help us to walk with you
as you walk with us. Amen.

The Questions

My Name Is . . .

• What do you know about how you got your name?

• What meaning does it hold for your family? For you?

Return to Oz

Sometimes it takes a wizard to tell us who we are. When I was growing up, *The Wizard of Oz* used to come on TV every year around Easter, which is very appropriate since I believe this is one of the most theologically-profound movies ever made. It has certainly helped me to see the good news. Its two big theological themes have to do with getting home and finding out who we are, both of which invite reflection on the vocational journey. Dorothy and her companions in Oz are all desperately seeking something they either have or have the ability to attain.

At the beginning of the movie, a tornado approaches; and Dorothy, the main character in the story, is trying desperately to get home. With the storm coming, everything Dorothy thought she knew is turned upside down. Dorothy has found her house, but the people who make it a home are not there. She's anxious about her life, her family, and the future. The tornado hits!

Dorothy's situation is similar to ours at times in our life. We have a home, we travel far from it, we lose our way, we forget who we were made and called to be, and when we try to get back on our own power we inevitably fail. In the end, we are carried off by forces much larger than we are, and it seems as if we'll never find home again.

Dorothy's house is thrown up into the air. She passes out. The house lands with a thud. She wakes up and goes cautiously to the door. She opens it up, and suddenly a flood of light enters the room. She has gone to the other side of the rainbow and it is a world of bright color and fascinating creatures. It turns out that her house has landed right on top of the wicked witch of the East, who has been cruelly oppressing the Munchkin people. Dorothy, as their liberator, is given a mysterious gift—the ruby slippers of the dead witch. She is toasted and sung to by all the Munchkins. But Dorothy knows that she needs to find some way to get home. What she doesn't know is that all she has to do is click the ruby slippers three times and say, "There's no place like home. There's no place like home. There's no place like home." But she hasn't been told this. She can't accept it at this moment. She has to take a journey.

So, she sets off down the yellow brick road in search of a wizard who can get her back home. Along the way she finds some companions, all of whom are as misguided as she is. First, there is the scarecrow that thinks he doesn't have a brain, even though in the first minutes she knows him he figures out how to get some nasty trees to throw them some apples and later hatches the plans that save the day. Then there is the tin man who thinks he doesn't have a heart, even though he is the most sentimental one in the bunch. And finally, there is the lion that thinks he has no courage, even though he is finally able to confront the witch of the West and the wizard.

Do you see the common theme here? Nobody knows who they are; and they all set off to see a wizard, who really isn't a wizard, to receive a reward that they already have. And along the way they have to overcome the witch of the West and her band of flying monkeys who threaten them with death and destruction. But the real obstacle in their journey is their inability to see who they really are.

In the closing scenes, it all becomes clear. The wizard plays an important role in helping these characters claim their gifts and abilities. Though he is captive to the expectations of the Emerald City's residents who have acclaimed him as a wizard, he is able to affirm the true strengths of those who have come to him. He recognizes the gifts the companions bring and gives them symbolic gifts: The scarecrow gets a diploma. The tin man gets a ticking red heart on a chain. The lion gets a medal. The wizard doesn't really give them anything that they don't already have. He gives them what they sought by helping them to see who they truly are. A little later Glenda, the good witch of the North, helps Dorothy realize that even she has the capacity she didn't think she had. She has the ability to go home by clicking her shoes.

I've had a few wizards grace my life through the years. I suspect you've had a few, too. They are the people in your life who help you see who you are and what you already have. They look very ordinary and they don't have any magical powers. But they speak to the place where God moves in our lives and helps us hear all over again just who we are. When we discover who we really are, we also discover that we are at home.

- If the companions already had the things that they sought from the wizard, what was the purpose of their journey?

- How do you understand the theme of going home? What does it mean to you?

- Symbolically speaking, what are the storms or tornadoes that unsettle your life?

- Who are the wizards in your life? Who has affirmed gifts that you already have so that you could claim them?

- If you were going to the wizard, what would you ask for?

The Scriptures

Samuel: God's Voice and a Mother's Prayer

Read 1 Samuel 1:9-18; 3:1-21.

Hannah was a woman who committed herself and her child to God before her child was even born. In a male-dominated society which placed a premium on the security a son could offer, Hannah prayed for a son, not for her own security, but so she could offer him to God. Hannah's song in 1 Samuel 2 is a hymn of celebration offered at the time when she gives Samuel, her son of promise, to be raised at the Shiloh temple by Eli. In it, she declares what God will do in the land.

Even though Hannah could see what God was up to, the text tells us that many others couldn't. "The word of the LORD was rare in those days," and even the priest Eli was unable to hear (3:1b). Samuel didn't recognize God's voice either in the early stages of this story, but eventually he heard a message that must have been very difficult for him to share with his surrogate father, Eli (3:10-14). Samuel's leadership as a prophet was marked by struggle and conflict; but despite the difficulties, he responded to the call of the God to whom his mother prayed and who called his name.

Samson: A Passionate Response, but to Whom?

Read Judges 13:1-7, 24; 14:1-20.

This may be a disturbing story for us. It comes out of a context that is very foreign to us. In ancient Israel, marriages between races were rare and women had very little autonomy. But we can recognize Samson. There are still Samsons among us who act out of their passions and who often react violently to conflicts.

Samson was dedicated to God before his birth. The Nazirite vows which the angel announced to his mother were signs that the child was to be set apart for a different kind of service to God. One of the expectations that came along with Samson's birth was that he was to lead the people out of oppression.

But Samson did not seem interested in the expectations of his parents. He took what he desired and displayed behavior that led to death and division. The passage talks about God's Spirit, but what Samson did seems far from what we expect.

Questions for Exploration

- To what is the child in each of these Scriptures committed before his birth?

- How does the child in each story respond to the expectations placed on him?

- Is there a conflict between the promise of the parent(s) and the will of the child? How do you see that at work in this story?

Your Reflections on the Scriptures

How do 1 Samuel 1:9-18; 3:1-21 and Judges 13:1-7, 24; 14:1-20 speak to your sense of vocation?

Your Life

"For you have made us for yourself, and our heart is restless until it rests in you."

—Saint Augustine

Augustine (354–430) was a bishop in northern Africa in the early Christian church. Looking back at his life in *The Confessions of Saint Augustine*, Augustine recognizes something very curious. Despite his many wanderings and failings, he was able to see a constant tugging within himself that kept moving him toward God. That tugging came in the midst of all sorts of relationships with people who asked different things of him. Augustine believed that our restless hearts are on a never-ending journey that is an expedition to seek God and our own true selves.

We Are Created to Be Related to God and Others.

- What difference does the knowledge that we are created to be related make in how we live out our lives and seek meaning?

Core Values and Your Life

What do the Core Values (page 8) say to you about the tensions between your inner sense of values and calling and the expectations others have for you?

Looking Ahead

• When you were a child, what did you want to be when you grew up?

• What does that early vision of vocation reveal about who you are?

• What values did you receive from family and others that inform who you are?

Closing Worship

Spirit of life,
who blesses us with water and moves our restless hearts,
you have created us to be related
to you and to the world.
As we begin this journey together,
bless to us our lives
so that we can see patterns of purpose
and respond to your relentless tuggings
filled with grace and love.
Amen.

2

Session Two
Passion and Vocation

Opening Prayer

God of the deep, rich earth,
you were not afraid to get your hands dirty
in bringing us forth from the mud of the ground.
Help us to be grounded in your love.
Christ who went below the waters,
you were not afraid to immerse yourself
and to invite us to follow you in baptism.
Let your love flow in us.
Spirit of wind and flame,
you were not afraid to spark a fire
and to give your people voice and power.
Burn within us with your purifying love.
Amen.

The Questions

What Is Passion?

In current usage, the word *passion* most often conjures up images of ardent love and romantic encounters; but other meanings of the word go deeper. When we speak of the passion of Christ, we speak about his suffering on behalf of and in solidarity with humanity. The passions of our souls are those things towards which we feel pulled. At its root, the word *passion* implies being acted upon by forces beyond ourselves and in that sense we can experience passion as suffering, longing, and love, all of which seem to be acting on us beyond our control at times. Discovering our *passion*, what our hearts truly desire, is one way to listen for God and to explore our vocation.

- How do you define *passion*?

- What are you *passionate* about?

- What connections do you see between *passion* and *vocation*?

The Beat in the Silence

Do you hear it?
The beat in the silence?
The sound at the center?
The voiceless cry of a soul seeking its author?
Do you hear it?
The beat, the beat.

Yes, you know
there is a beat, beat, beat,
there is purpose,
there is movement,
at the heart, heart, heart of it all.

For you praise waits in silence, O God *Elohim,*
blasting rock of our salvation.
For you praise waits
like a beast whose calling I do not yet hear,

like smoke rising from an unacknowledged sacrifice,
for you praise waits, waits, waits,
impatiently,
in steadfast restlessness,
ready to leap forth like a big cat stalking its prey,
hungry, yearning, caged by silence, silence, silence,
yet all that is within me wants to sing,
all that is within me wants to praise you, Lord.
To you we will offer our vows,
to you all flesh shall come,
for you praise waits, waits, waits,
it is the passion implanted in me
before my mother knew me,
before the dawn of my dawns,
before before.

Praise waits
in ranting, urgent, edgy, unsung tones
growling, purring, tensed,
and ready to pounce back to its Maker
like fire in my bones,
a thanks to be given,
a cry to be released,
a bell to be rung.

Yes, you know.

At the core of my being,
at the center of my self,
at the heart of every nucleus,
there is a tone, a sound, a beat, an energy,
a unique marker
unduplicated in all the passing
of every bygone age

like a GPS signal to the great unknown,
like an echo of some half-remembered phrase in a like voice,
like you, like me, there is a tone, a sound,
a beat, a beat, a beat,
there's within my heart a melody,
and let those who have ears to hear listen
to what the Spirit is saying
O yes, you know.

The beat, the beat, the beat.
I did not know this song.
I only came to hum a few bars.
I only poked my head in because the music sounded sweet.
I only sang the melody because it had a catchy hook.
I did not know it was my song.
I did not know praise waits, waits, waits.
I did not know this God *Elohim*.
I do not know this God right now
but somehow God knows me.
In some messed up, straightened out, mind-blowing, heartbreaking
harmony,
creation is singing my note,
and my note sings with sheep and hills and stones and grain,
and my note is my own, and yet it is God's.

For you praise waits in silence, O God *Elohim*,
ever-loving river that is God
for you praise waits, waits, waits,
and yet all around me creation speaks, whispers, breathes, sighs,
groans, howls, cries out, shouts, celebrates.
How can I keep from singing?
Shall I sit caged in silence, starving, music-less?
Shall stones cry out on my behalf?
Shall grazing, mute, grass-muzzled sheep
speak your name more gloriously than I?

Shall gurgling streams and foul tempests of the seas
take my place in the chorus?
Shall I not speak and cry and howl?
Shall I not shout and sing for joy?
Shall I let grain-filled valleys interrupt my praise?
Shall I let hills be more alive with the sound of music
than the depths of my ever-loving soul?
Yes, you know,
down in the deeps of the earth
there is a song
waiting to be released,
a great frolicking beast ready to spring forth from a cage of silence

Yes, you know
Praise waits in silence.
All you have to do
is let it go.

—Alex Joyner

- What images or ideas stand out for you in the poem?

- What does the idea of a beat in the silence suggest to you?

- What connections do you see between praise of God and passion?

• How does this poem speak to you about knowledge of self, of God, and of vocation?

The Scriptures

The Psalms are filled with emotion and passion. Psalm 65 reminds us that praise is the most natural language of creation. Read these verses aloud. Underline words that have meaning for you. Read the entire psalm.

> Happy are those whom you choose and bring near
> to live in your courts.
> We shall be satisfied with the goodness of your house,
> your holy temple.
> By awesome deeds you answer us with deliverance,
> O God of our salvation;
> you are the hope of all the ends of the earth
> and of the farthest seas.
> —Psalm 65:4-5

Your Reflections on the Scriptures

How does Psalm 65 speak to you as you think about passion and vocation?

Your Life

Ambition:

Desire to achieve a particular end
> —*Merriam-Webster's Online Dictionary* (2006–07)

• How is God speaking through your ambition?

Vocation:

"Vocation speaks of a gracious discovery of a kind of interior consonance between our deepest desires and hopes and our unique gifts, as they are summoned forth by the needs of others and realized in response to that summons."[1]

> —Brian Mahan

• What surprises you about this understanding of vocation?

• According to the quotation above, what things come together when we discover our vocation? What calls them forth?

• How is God speaking through this understanding of vocation?

• How are ambition and vocation different?

• Our passions are important because . . .

• Draw an image of your passion in the space below:

Core Values and Your Life

What do the Core Values (page 8) say to you about your passion and vocation?

Looking Ahead

Catch Yourself Being Yourself

When our minds start to wander when we're trying to focus on something, we usually think of this as a bad thing. This week it's a good thing because it offers you the chance to catch yourself being yourself. Our distractions can sometimes tell us what's really important to us. In an exercise suggested by Brian Mahan, keep this journal handy as you go through the week and when you find your mind wandering.[2] What are you really thinking about as you are reading a book, sitting in class, or waiting for an appointment? Write it down quickly in the distraction diary below.

Distraction Diary:

What I'm really thinking about is . . .

What I'm really thinking about is . . .

What I'm really thinking about is . . .

Return to your distraction diary at the end of the day and ask yourself these questions:

• What are my distractions telling me about what is important to me?

• What passions are moving me?

• How could God be speaking through these distractions?

Closing Worship

The word I'm hearing right now is _____.

Spirit of life,
who blesses us with water and moves our restless hearts,
our passions burn within us.
Hear these words that sound in our souls:

[*Reflect silently on the word you wrote above. Conclude:*]

For you praise waits in silence, God.
Let us join the chorus
and respond to your relentless tuggings
filled with joy.
Amen.

---

[1] *Forgetting Ourselves on Purpose: Vocation and the Ethics of Ambition,* by Brian J. Mahan (Jossey-Bass, 2002); pages 10–11.
[2] Mahan; pages 34–37.

3

Session Three
Trusting the Gifts

Opening Prayer

God of migrant wanderers,
our minds drift and slip and flow
from passionate awareness of your presence
to forgetfulness and fear.
Bless to us this day our lives
that we may follow where Abraham and Sarah once did,
out from the comfortable places where we hang out
to the new territories where we can live
with you.
Amen.

The Questions

Vera and the Storm

Vera was right. Her parents freaked out when they learned that she was going to Nicaragua for a beach trip with her best friend, Gabriella, and some other friends from school. "Nicaragua?!," they had said. "Why Nicaragua?!" They also seemed fairly dissatisfied with Vera's response: "Why not?" But on the plane ride down even she wondered why she had agreed to this crazy trip. She didn't know any Spanish! Her 200-level French was not going to help her here.

What she hadn't anticipated was how everything seemed to change for her after her last exam. The semester had felt like a huge steamroller bearing down on her so that she had to keep running every second to avoid being flattened. There wasn't much room to think about the summer, her parents, the beach trip, or even how she was feeling. But as she turned in her last exam, a strange mixture of relief and apprehension settled in.

She was definitely feeling better with the steamroller fading into the distance behind her. But in the pit of her stomach, she also felt

40

a sense of foreboding and instability that she hadn't had since her first days at college when she was wondering if she had made the right choice in coming to school at all.

Gabriella, who was sitting next to her on the plane, noticed that Vera was a little preoccupied. "So, what's up?"

"Gabriella, do you know what you're going to do when you grow up?"

"Hey, what's to say I'm not grown up already?"

"O.K., yeah, but I mean, what next? After college."

"No clue, Vera."

"I don't have a clue, either. I don't know who I'm supposed to be. I mean, at home I never thought about it. I never had much of a goal besides going to college. When classes are going, it's easy—I'm a student. And I'm learning to do so many things. But here I am going to another country, and I'm going to hand over my passport and they're going to say, 'Welcome, Vera Allen,' and I don't know who that is!"

"So, it's about going to another country?"

"No, Gabby it has nothing to do with another country. I don't know who Vera Allen is in the United States! I don't know what I'm doing or where I'm headed. I don't know who or what to trust. I don't know who God wants me to be. And it feels like freedom, but it also feels, like . . . really scary."

They landed without incident at a small, one-runway airport at the edge of a vast jungle. The group boarded a taxi to head to the hotel where they were staying. "Taxi" is a generous description. It was a pick-up truck with rough wooden benches fixed over each wheel base. The "hotel" was a collection of cinderblock cabanas facing the ocean. A larger cinderblock building with a timber roof served as the office, restaurant, and local health clinic. It was the most substantial building in a very small city. A friendly, elderly couple showed them their rooms and then left them there.

The students threw their bags down and headed straight for the beach. It was warm and wonderful—very different from what they had left behind, but a stiff wind was blowing off of the ocean. The setting sun was soon obscured by a raft of dark, billowy clouds on the horizon. Before long the atmosphere was as unsettled as Vera felt. A big storm was coming. The group returned to their rooms. When Vera peeked out at the ocean, it was seething and tossing huge waves. The students escaped to the larger building where the hotel guests were gathered. Vera plopped down on the floor and leaned against a wall. Gabriella joined her.

"So . . . want to play some cards?"

"No, Gabriella. Thanks, but I just don't think I could concentrate."

"Well, you could watch the storm." She said. "Storms are great!"

"Storms are not 'great.' They're big and scary and they knock lots of stuff down."

"So, what do you want to do, Vera?"

"I want to get out of here. I want to go home. I want to pray. I want to figure out what to do with my life. I don't know. My life feels just like that storm!"

- What is making Vera anxious in the story?

- How does Gabriella respond to her? With whom do you most identify, Vera or Gabriella? Why?

- How does the storm reflect Vera's mood?

- Does being away from home or being in a storm describe your feelings about vocation? Why or why not?

The Scriptures

Imagine yourself as both Martha and Mary in Luke 10:38-42.

NARRATOR: Now as they went on their way, Jesus entered a certain village, where a woman named Martha welcomed him into her home. She had a sister named Mary, who sat at the Lord's feet and listened to what he was saying. But Martha was distracted by her many tasks; so she came to him and asked:

MARTHA: "Lord, do you not care that my sister has left me all the work to do by myself? Tell her then to help me."

JESUS: "Martha, Martha, you are worried and distracted by many things; there is need of only one thing. Mary has chosen the better part, which will not be taken away from her."

—Luke 10:38-42, adapted

First as Mary, then as Martha, respond to the following questions:

• What was your response when you realized that Jesus was coming to your house?

• What did you hear Jesus saying to you while he was here?

Your Reflections on the Scriptures

How does the story of Martha and Mary in Luke 10:38-42 speak to you about the anxieties of vocation? About trusting our gifts?

Your Life

The Tree and the Wind

Imagine that you are a tree being blown by the wind. Describe yourself in the space below:

Imagine that you are the wind. Describe yourself in the space below:

- *I recognize the tree in me when I . . .*

- *I recognize the wind in me when I . . .*

Core Values and Your Life

What do the Core Values (page 8) say to you about the anxieties of vocation? About trusting our gifts?

Looking Ahead

The Parts That Need Changing

Use this week to construct a spiritual autobiography in the space provided on the following page. In whatever way seems most natural to you (story, timeline, images, photos), tell the story of your life with God. What are the marker events that deepened your relationship with God? When were the times you felt furthest away? When you have finished the autobiography project, ask yourself:

- What had to change in me at each of those moments when I grew closer to God?

- What needs to change in me now for me to grow closer to God?

MY SPIRITUAL AUTOBIOGRAPHY

Closing Worship

Breathing In, Breathing Out

When Paul told the Christians of Thessalonica that they should "pray without ceasing," he left us with a model of prayer that many find difficult (1 Thessalonians 5:17). How are we to pray without ceasing?

The desert mystics of the fourth century developed a form of prayer that was tied to breathing. By taking short phrases that could be whispered as they are breathed in and out, these searchers after God developed a prayer life that kept them close to the source of their life in the midst of very challenging conditions. The most famous of these is the Jesus Prayer that uses the phrase, "Lord Jesus Christ, Son of God, have mercy on me, a sinner."

The breath prayer is a spiritual exercise that can help us trust what God is doing with us and in us. Pray the following sentence as a breath prayer each day during the week ahead: "Jesus, lover of my soul, you alone are all I need."

Jesus, Lover of our souls,
you call us from the craziness of our days
to discover the one thing we need to live.
As the men and women who were your disciples
left behind what they knew
to become what they would be,
so let us walk in your way,
share in your joy,
and dance in your love.
Amen.

Session Four
Listening in the Shadows

Opening Prayer

Spirit, moving in my soul,
you uncover my thoughts
and trouble my self-deceptions.
Disturb me
like a field is prepared for planting
and open my heart to grow.
Spirit, moving in my soul,
wash me,
cleanse me,
make me whole. Amen.

The Questions

I Have to Take This Call

A young man walks beside a river on a beautiful day. He speaks aloud to no one in particular, "Not a care in the world. Watching this lazy river flow on by. It's easy to believe that God is good on a day like today." His cell phone rings. "I have to take this call," he says. The call is from God. Listen to the young man's side of the conversation. He is aware of his weaknesses, deficiencies, and hidden longings. Through the course of the conversation, he realizes that these may be the very places in his life where God is bringing about transformation.

"Yes? God?" He is surprised, but continues the conversation. "Well, I'm sitting here enjoying this fine day you've given us and . . . why am I telling you this? You know what I'm doing! Of course I'm at ease. You did what? You left something at my house for me? Some affirmations for me? Well, thank you. You're always sending me stuff I don't deserve. Where'd you leave them? In the closet? Which closet?"

The young man's face falls as he hears the answer to this question, and he becomes agitated.

"Oh . . . *that* closet. Well, I didn't know you knew about that. Well, of course—you know what I'm doing, you know about the closet. It's just that . . . well, I'm not too proud of that closet. It's a mess. Yeah, I know. You KNOW it's a mess."

"So where in the closet did you leave the, uh, affirmations? On the green box? Oh, yeah . . . *that* box. No, no, that's cool, God. I guess you knew I had a box labeled, "Major-League Anxieties." Yeah, that's where I keep my Can-I-Pay-My-Credit-Card concerns and my Will-She-Think-I'm-Stupid suspicions and my Do-I-Have-What-It-Takes apprehensions. So, uh, that's it, God? You didn't leave me anything . . . else?

"On the red box, too? Oh, yeah. You saw that one, too, God. Yeah, the old Trunk of Trepidations. I've been keeping that one around for a long time. I keep my Social Distresses and Depression Impressions in there. What's that? Yes, God. And the picture from my senior prom. Hey, you didn't go snooping around too much in that closet, did you, because there's some stuff that's pretty fragile . . . Oh, you saw that, too?

"Well, the yellow box is where I keep those, uh . . . Hidden Desires. No, I'm not ashamed of them, I'm just . . . kind of afraid of them. Yes, afraid. What would people say if they knew I was so idealistic? They would think I was a freak if I told them what I really wanted. And I'm not sure I'd like what I'd have to change if I really listened to them. So I tuck the desires away in that box. Now next to that . . .

"Of course you found that, too. That's the Wardrobe of Worries. Yeah, I know I'm gifted. People keep telling me that. But what if they're wrong? What if I'm not really all that great at loving other people? What if I am not such the awesome person I think I am? What if I shouldn't put all my eggs into one basket? I keep a few in that wardrobe. No, not literal eggs. I mean, like, parts of me. No, not like an arm. I mean like the places in me that I don't want to get hurt. The stuff I've got to protect from disappointment and discouragement and disaster. The worries. I kind of like that wardrobe. And I keep it in front of . . . .

"Oh, you found that, too?" His tone turns much more serious. "Well, it's just a small thing really. Just big enough to keep Niggling Doubts. Things like Hurtful-Things-My-Parents-Told-Me and People-Who-Let-Me-Down and Secrets-I-Won't-Tell-Anyone. You didn't, uh . . . you didn't *open* that one did you, God? You put an affirmation in there! Well, that means I've got to open it up to get it out! I'm not going in there, God. You don't know what those things do to me! I've been hurt way too many times opening that chest. You know, I can handle the Wardrobe of Worries and the Trunk of Trepidations and even the Major-League Anxieties, but those Niggling Doubts are nasty! I just want to leave them behind. No good can come from going back to them.

"You did what? You left the most important affirmation there?! In the Chest of Niggling Doubts?! Well, yes, you know I want to follow you. Yes, I know. Yes! I said that I would hand over everything to you. All that I am is yours, and from you no secrets are hidden . . . no closets are untouched.

"No, I'm not trying to hold something back, it's just that . . . well, those parts of me are unworthy of . . . of you! What's that? Who made those parts of me? Don't pull rank on me now, God. That just doesn't make sense. I can see how you show me who I am by revealing my gifts and talents and friends and guides and dreams and visions. I get that, God. But my worries and doubts and anxieties and hidden desires? What could you possibly do with them?

"Yes, I guess you could speak to me through them. Yes, I'll check as soon as I get home." He continues somewhat hesitantly. "If you left me something . . . it's got to be good. Yeah, I love you, too. Thanks."

What Do You Keep in Your . . .

Box of Major-League Anxieties?

Trunk of Trepidations?

Box of Hidden Desires?

Wardrobe of Worries?

Chest of Niggling Doubts?

The Scriptures

Bent Over No More

Read Luke 13:10-17. Write responses to the following questions:

• What does the world look like when you can only look down?

• If this were the first time you looked straight ahead in 18 years, how would you feel?

• What would you be likely to notice?

• Who are you? The bent-over woman, the healed woman, one of the rule-keepers, or someone else in the story? Why?

Your Reflections on the Scriptures

How does the story of the bent-over woman in Luke 13:10-17 speak to you about listening to God in the shadows and experiencing God's transformation?

Your Life

Draw the place in your life that most needs to be changed or healed.

Core Values and Your Life

What do the Core Values (page 8) say to you about listening to God in the shadows and experiencing God's transformation?

Looking Ahead

Moving Out

There's a whole world out there, and it's calling your name! This week, go out and meet it. There are places in your community that are looking for volunteers to help meet the needs of underserved people. Food banks, schools, home repair groups, community organizing projects, and many other organizations have opportunities to help others. Perhaps you already participate in some of these.

Before the next session, spend some time helping someone else. In fact, make it a habit! Remember that "we are created to be related to God and others." If you need some help getting started, talk with your group leader about possibilities in your area. Or get together with some other members of the group and head out together. Try to participate in an activity this week. If for some reason you cannot, you may use an experience of service in the past for reflection. Write about what the experience was like for you. Ask yourself:

• When did I feel most comfortable?

• When did I feel most uncomfortable?

• What happened during the experience that I want to remember?

• What did I learn about myself?

LISTENING IN THE SHADOWS

• What needs of the world do I feel most called to address?

• What gifts do I have to offer the world?

Closing Worship

Remold Me, Make Me

My symbol of healing looks like . . .

Don't invite God in if you don't want to change!

Spirit, moving in my soul,
I open my hands
and know they are scarred.
I open my eyes
and know they often stray.
I open my heart
and know it can love more.
I open my life
and ask you to come in.
Remold me.
Make me yours. Amen.

5

Session Five
Somebody's Calling Your Name

Opening Prayer

Jesus, you met a woman at a well
and asked for something to drink.
At wells and watering holes, your people gather
sometimes thirsty,
sometimes dusty,
sometimes longing for a splash of something cool.
We come to this water today
because our skin is too dry
and our souls too parched
for want of your love.
With all your thirsting children,
we wait for you here. Amen.

The Questions

I Want to Hear My True Name

Devon is talking to a friend in line at the coffee shop. Listen to what he says about names.

I was in here last week, and I put in my order like I always do. Grande skinny half-caf latte, hold the whipped cream. Hey, what can I say? I'm not as extreme as I look. Anyway, there was a new girl behind the espresso machine and she doesn't know me so she doesn't know that my name is De-VON. De-VON. Is that so hard?

So when my drink was ready she said, "DEV-on. Your grande skinny half-caf latte no cream is up." And I am sooo ready to go and tell her where to get off but when I get up there, I get it together, look at her nametag, and I just say, "Hey, thanks . . . Laurie. And by the way, it's, uh, De-VON." I was so smooth. I don't think she even noticed when I tripped over the chair on the way out the door. Today . . . she's back. And I'm betting she remembers.

So here's the thing about names: They're important! I heard this story one time about a rabbi in Prague—Rabbi Yehuda Loew ben Bezalel. Quite a name, huh? He was the most famous rabbi of his day. People knew him because he had created the Golem, the form of a man made out of clay that he gave life to by putting the name of God on a slip of paper under its tongue. Or so the story goes.

Anyway, one night Rabbi Yehuda had a dream. He dreamed that he had died and was brought before the throne of God. An angel came out and said, "Who are you?"

"I am Rabbi Yehuda, the creator of the Golem," he said. He figured surely they would know him by that. That's how everybody else knew him.

But the angel said, "Wait here. I'm going to read the names of everyone who has died this day whose names are in the book." The angel opened the book and started to read. And as the angel read names, spirits started to respond and to fly into the glory above the throne.

Rabbi Yehuda waited and waited, but when the angel finished reading, he was still sitting there. He started to cry and yell at the angel.

The angel looked at him and said, "Why are you crying out? I have called your name."

"Well, I didn't hear it!"

"In this book are the names of every man and woman who ever lived on earth, because every soul has a share in the Kingdom," the angel said. "But, you know, many times people come who have never heard their true names on the lips of humans or angels. They thought they knew their names, but they didn't. So they don't recognize their true names when they are called. They don't recognize that the gates of the Kingdom are open for them. So they have to wait here until they hear their names and know them. Maybe once in their life one person called them by their right name. They have to sit here until they can remember it. Maybe no one has ever called

65

WHERE DO I GO NOW, GOD?

them by their right name. Here they stay until they are quiet enough to hear the King of the Universe calling them."

Well, at this, Rabbi Yehuda woke up from his dream with tears streaming down his face. He got out of bed, covered his head, lay prostrate on the ground, and he prayed, "Master of the Universe! Grant me once before I die to hear my own true name on the lips of my brothers or sisters."[1]

Man, that really gets to me. I want to hear my true name! Oh. It's my turn to order . . . "Hi, uh, Laurie, right?"

The quotations below tell us that both Devon and Rabbi Yehuda want to hear their true names. Have you had similar experiences? Write about them in the space after the quotations.

"De-VON. De-VON. Is that so hard?"

"Master of the Universe! Grant me once before I die to hear my own true name on the lips of my brothers or sisters."

• What is different about the true names that Devon and Rabbi Yehuda want to hear?

• What do you think keeps us from hearing our "true" names?

The Scriptures

Isaiah 58:1-12

Fasting

The people of Israel fasted as a sign of repentance when they were seeking to restore their relationship with God. Jesus began his ministry with fasting in the wilderness and taught his disciples to join fasting and prayer. The early church set aside regular days for fasting each week. Usually, fasting involves foregoing solid food for a certain period. The intent is to open ourselves to what God is doing in us and in the world. The point of fasting is not to prove our ability to withstand hunger pangs but to connect us more deeply to God.

Lauren Winner, in her book *Mudhouse Sabbath*, talks about her struggles to fast while living the life of a contemporary young adult in America. She recalls asking a rabbi about how hunger could be helpful to her spiritual life. His response was, "When you are fasting and you feel hungry, you are to remember that you are really hungry for God."[2]

• What does it mean to you to be hungry for God?

A Responsive Reading

This passage from Isaiah gives us a prophet's warning to a culture that was also confused about fasting. God's people were confused about a practice that was intended to help persons restore a right relationship with God, to open them to God's continued work in them, and to remind them of their soul's desire for God. Isaiah calls the people to understand their fast as an opening to right action as well. The people were very good at observing the fast, but they failed to live out a God-centered life in their relations with other people, particularly with the poor. The fast God requires is not an individual exercise in self-improvement, but a communal experience of peace making and justice.

A: Shout out, do not hold back!/ Lift up your voice like a trumpet!

B: Announce to my people their rebellion,/ to the house of Jacob their sins.

A: Yet day after day they seek me/ and delight to know my ways,

B: as if they were a nation that practiced righteousness/ and did not forsake the ordinance of their God;

A: they ask of me righteous judgments,/ they delight to draw near to God.

B: "Why do we fast, but you do not see?/ Why humble ourselves, but you do not notice?"

A: Look, you serve your own interest on your fast day,/ and oppress all your workers.

B: Look, you fast only to quarrel and to fight/ and to strike with a wicked fist.

A: Such fasting as you do today/ will not make your voice heard on high.

B: Is such the fast that I choose,/ a day to humble oneself?

A: Is it to bow down the head like a bulrush,/ and to lie in sackcloth and ashes?

B: Will you call this a fast,/ a day acceptable to the LORD?

A: Is not this the fast that I choose:/ to loose the bonds of injustice,/ to undo the thongs of the yoke,

B: to let the oppressed go free,/ and to break every yoke?

A: Is it not to share your bread with the hungry,/ and bring the homeless poor into your house;

B: when you see the naked, to cover them,/ and not to hide yourself from your own kin?

A: Then your light shall break forth like the dawn,/ and your healing shall spring up quickly;

B: your vindicator shall go before you,/ the glory of the LORD shall be your rear guard.

A: Then you shall call, and the LORD will answer;/ you shall cry for help, and he will say, Here I am.

B: If you remove the yoke from among you,/ the pointing of the finger, the speaking of evil,

A: if you offer your food to the hungry/ and satisfy the needs of the afflicted,

B: then your light shall rise in the darkness/ and your gloom be like the noonday.

A: The LORD will guide you continually,/ and satisfy your needs in parched places,/ and make your bones strong;

B: and you shall be like a watered garden,/ like a spring of water,/ whose waters never fail.

A: Your ancient ruins shall be rebuilt;/ you shall raise up the foundations of many generations;

B: you shall be called the repairer of the breach,/ the restorer of streets to live in.

Matthew 25:31-46

Jesus told his followers that they would see him in the "least of these my brothers and sisters" (Matthew 25:40, NLT). We are also invited to meet Jesus in marginalized people and places. Think about your community, the nation, and the world. Who would you identify as the "least of these"? Read Matthew 25:31-46. Write about your insights or paste pictures in the space below that illustrate "the least of these."

SOMEBODY'S CALLING YOUR NAME

Your Reflections on the Scriptures

How do Isaiah 58:1-12 and Matthew 25:31-46 speak to you about your true name, your vocation, and the needs of the world?

71

Your Life

"The place God calls you to is the place where your deep gladness and the world's deep hunger meet."[3]

—Frederick Buechner

Compassion and Justice

In interpreting John Wesley's call for his small groups to pursue acts of mercy, the Covenant Discipleship model distinguishes between acts of compassion and acts of justice, both of which are acts of mercy. *Compassion* is what we express when we offer help to a neighbor in a time of obvious need. A person who gives food to a hungry person or provides medical care to someone who is sick is responding with compassion. *Justice* goes beyond compassion to ask why there are continuing situations of need in our communities and in the world. Reflecting on the causes of injustice, Christians respond by seeking to change the things that lead to suffering and inequity.[4] In the space provided below, write about specific examples of compassion and justice.

COMPASSION: Acts of compassion are immediate responses to obvious needs.

JUSTICE: Acts of justice address the causes of suffering, need, and inequity.

Core Values and Your Life

What do the Core Values (page 8) say to you about your true name, your vocation, and the needs of the world?

Looking Ahead

Getting It Down on Paper

When we are in the midst of busy schedules or occupied with other activities, it is easy to lose track of important thoughts that come to us. At those times we may say, "I've got to get this down on paper!"

As we move to the close of this study, it is important that we get down on paper what we have been learning about who we are and what God is calling us to be. Through this week, use the incomplete sentences below to help you sort through the journey you have been on. If you are beginning to get a vision of a specific calling, put that down as well. Remember that your responses do not have to be in complete sentences. God may be speaking to you through phrases, words, poems, or images.

To really know me, you need to know that I . . .

The place in my life where God is most at work is . . .

The needs of the world that are calling my name are . . .

When I imagine myself ten years from now, I see . . .

Over the weeks of this study, the new vision God has given me of who I am is . . .

Closing Worship

Name Calling

_____, God is blessing you and calling your name.

God, who whispers in the night
and shouts in the bright sunshine of creation's glory,
don't let my ears be closed,
don't let my eyes be shut,
don't let my heart be hardened,
don't let my hands be clenched,
but let me be open, ready, willing, and able
to hear my name
and to answer your call. Amen.

---

[1] The Rabbi Yehuda story is based on a retelling of the legend in *A Ray of Darkness: Sermons and Reflections,* by Rowan Williams (Cowley Publications, 1995); pages 152–53.
[2] *Mudhouse Sabbath,* by Lauren F. Winner (Paraclete Press, 2003); pages 90–91.
[3] *Wishful Thinking: A Seeker's ABC,* by Frederick Buechner (HarperSanFrancisco, 1993); page 119.
[4] For more information on the Covenant Discipleship movement, visit the website of The United Methodist Church's General Board of Discipleship at: http://www.gbod.org/smallgroup/cd/. Or see the book, *Guide for Covenant Discipleship Groups,* by Gayle Turner Watson (Discipleship Resources, 2000). Another resource designed for youth and college students is *Together in Love: Covenant Discipleship for Youth,* by David C. Sutherland (Discipleship Resources, 1999).

6

Session Six
Taking Risks

Opening Prayer

A voice calls in the wilderness,
"Come, discover your salvation at the margins."
And so we come to live on the edge.
Believing that God is able,
that Christ is sufficient,
that the Spirit is moving across the face of the waters,
we come to live on the edge
of a new and promised day.
Amen.

The Questions

Risky Behavior

Just how do you feel about risky behavior? Stating the question this way gives it a pejorative tone. Parents, school counselors, or law enforcement personnel encourage young adults *not* to engage in risky behavior—anything that could lead them to harm or trouble. We have programs promoting the use of helmets for skateboarders and cyclists. We educate persons about the dangers of unprotected sexual activity. We teach about the ill consequences of drug and alcohol abuse. Businesses create whole departments of risk management. Financial analysts and insurance adjustors plot the economic cost of risk. Politicians hide their true convictions if they are not in tune with focus groups and surveys.

Young adults are no strangers to risk. From impetuous decisions to extreme sports, risk seems to be a natural part of life. Along with the adventure, though, caution has not been completely thrown to the wind. Kite boarding may not seem scary, but exposing feelings to another person can be terrifying. Claiming an ideal or professing faith publicly can feel extremely threatening.

It is good to be cautious with behaviors that might harm us or others. Risky behavior, however, may have positive results. In fact, it is a hallmark of the Christian life. Many biblical people took great risks in their response to God. Abram and Sarai packed up all they had and left their family behind to follow God's promise and call. Ruth left Moab for a dubious future with a grieving mother-in-law. Disciples dropped fishing nets. Prophets called the political and religious leadership to accountability. Paul, a persecutor of Christians, became an unlikely apostle of the good news of Christ. Clearly, these folks never received lessons in risk management!

Let's go back to the initial question: How do you feel about risky behavior? Write responses to the questions below.

• What comes to mind when you hear the phrase "risky behavior"?

• How do you respond to the idea that risky behavior is a hallmark of Christian life? In what sense might this be true?

• What risky behaviors might have positive results?

The Scriptures

Ruth and Risk

But Ruth said,
"Do not press me to leave you
   or to turn back from following you!
Where you go, I will go;
   where you lodge, I will lodge;
your people shall be my people,
   and your God my God.
Where you die, I will die—
   there will I be buried.
May the LORD do thus and so to me,
   and more as well,
if even death parts me from you!"
              —Ruth 1:16-17

    The biblical story of Ruth is often seen as a tale of deep friendship and covenantal love. In Ruth's pledge to her mother-in-law, Naomi, we hear echoes of the sort of love God calls us to have for each other and echoes of the kind of love God has for us. But digging deeper into the biblical tale we find a story fraught with contingency and risk. Ruth leaves behind the relative security of her native land, Moab, to accompany Naomi, who, as a landless widow, would have no security even in her own land.

    Later in the story, Ruth finds herself in situations that highlight her vulnerability. She goes to glean among the harvesters to provide food for Naomi and herself, despite the fact that the fields were often very dangerous places for women. Later, she goes to the threshing floor at night, a place with a very dubious reputation in Scripture (see Hosea 9:1). There, Ruth challenges Boaz, the field owner and Naomi's near kinsman, to redeem their situation. Again, she places herself at great personal risk.

The message of the story is not a simple one of friendship and trust. Here we also find difficult choices and the willingness of a young woman to stretch into the unknown with a God whom she is only beginning to know.

• What is Naomi's most compelling reason for returning home?

• Why does Naomi press Orpah and Ruth to return home?

• Why might Orpah and Ruth want to go with Naomi?

• What risks was Ruth taking in making her pledge to Naomi?

Your Reflections on the Scriptures

How does the Book of Ruth speak to you about risk? About trusting God? About God's call in your life?

Your Life

Draw or write about a new vision of yourself given to you by God through this study.

An Action Plan

The Next Step

The most important thing I have discovered about who God is calling me to be is . . .

If I believe this vision to be true, then I will . . .

So, by this date: _____,

I will _____

_____,

trusting that God will meet me in the next step.

Signed, _____

Date: _____

Core Values and Your Life

How do the Core Values (page 8) speak to you about risk and about trusting God as you pursue a vision of your vocation?

Looking Ahead

Emmanuel Cardinal Suhard wrote that the Christian life "means to live in such a way that one's life would not make sense if God did not exist."[1] Steve Long, associate professor of theology at Garrett-Evangelical Theological Seminary, adapted this statement as he spoke to a group of young people exploring ordained ministry when he challenged them "to live in such a way that your life would not make sense if the gospel you proclaim is not true."[2] A truth claim resides in the decisions we make about how we live our lives and to which things we give ourselves. Living a truth claim always involves risk. Read the sentence below. Consider what difference it might make in your life.

Live your life in such a way that it would not make sense
if the gospel were not true.

Closing Worship

Retrieving the Stones

You have not traveled alone on this journey of vocational reflection. You have traveled with God and other people. Write the names of all the companions who have traveled with you in this study. Beside each name, write the blessing they have brought to the group.

NAMES of companions   BLESSINGS they have brought

God of Ruth and Naomi,
you bind together unlikely folks
and bless them in the midst of their uncertainty.
Christ of the table and the cross,
you take the places
where we are blessed and where we curse
and fashion them into instruments of our new identity.
Spirit moving across the waters of creation,
you claim us and call us,
so that we can live on the edge
of what you will do in us today.
Thank you. Amen.

---

[1] Emmanuel Cardinal Suhard, Archbishop of Paris, quoted in "Revolutionary of the Heart," by Geoffrey B. Gneuhs, *First Things* (May 1998); available at: http://www.firstthings.com/article.php3?id_article=3517.
[2] From an address given by Steve Long at "Exploration 2000" held in Dallas, TX, Nov. 11–12, 2000.